D0535726

CHIPMUNKS

ANIMALS UNDERGROUND

EMILY SEBASTIAN

PowerKiDS press™

New York

Published in 2012 by The Rosen Publishing Group, Inc.
29 East 21st Street, New York, NY 10010

First Edition

Editor: Amelie von Zumbusch
Book Design: Julio Gil

Photo Credits: Cover James Hager/Robert Harding World Imagery/Getty Images; back cover (armadillo, fox, mongoose), pp. 5, 6–7, 8–9, 11, 12–13, 15, 21, 23, 24 (top right, bottom right) Shutterstock.com; back cover (badger) Norbert Rosing/National Geographic/Getty Images; back cover (mole) Geoff du Feu/Stone/Getty Images; pp. 16–17, 24 (bottom left) Tohoku Color Agency/Japan Images/Getty Images; pp. 19, 24 (top left) Frank Cezus/Taxi/Getty Images.

Library of Congress Cataloging-in-Publication Data

Sebastian, Emily.
Chipmunks / by Emily Sebastian. — 1st ed.
    p. cm. — (Animals underground)
Includes index.
ISBN 978-1-4488-4954-3 (library binding) — ISBN 978-1-4488-5058-7 (pbk.) —
ISBN 978-1-4488-5059-4 (6-pack)
1. Chipmunks—Juvenile literature. I. Title.
QL737.R68S43 2012
599.36'4—dc22
                                          2010050934

Manufactured in the United States of America

CPSIA Compliance Information: Batch #WS11PK: For Further Information contact Rosen Publishing, New York, New York at 1-800-237-9932

CONTENTS

Chipmunks are cute! They are part of the squirrel family.

One kind of chipmunk lives in Asia. The rest live in North America.

Chipmunks are small. Bigger animals, such as **owls**, eat chipmunks.

Chipmunks make a sound when they are in danger. It sounds like "chip, chip, chip."

Baby chipmunks live with their mothers. Older chipmunks live alone.

Seeds and nuts are a chipmunk's main foods. Chipmunks store food to eat later.

Chipmunks gather most of their food on the ground. They also climb trees to reach food.

Most chipmunks dig **burrows**. These have many chambers, or rooms.

Chipmunks stuff their **cheeks** full of food. This is how they carry food around.

Chipmunks sleep most of the winter. They wake up to eat, though.

Words to Know

burrow

climb

cheeks

owl

Web Sites

Due to the changing nature of Internet links, PowerKids Press has developed an online list of Web sites related to the subject of this book. This site is updated regularly. Please use this link to access the list:
www.powerkidslinks.com/anun/chipmunk/